BUDGETING BASIC

Get Your Finances in Order Once & For All

Kennisha Pressley-Smith

KPS Real Investment

CONTENTS

ABOUT THE AUTHOR

Greetings, I'm Kennisha Pressley-Smith, a seasoned finance professional boasting over a decade of expertise in the field. My dedication lies in empowering individuals to seize command of their financial destinies and reach their monetary objectives. Having collaborated with clients from diverse backgrounds, I comprehend the distinct hurdles faced by underrepresented communities. My mission is to foster more inclusive access to financial education and resources.

In my role as a financial planner and educator, I've witnessed firsthand the transformative influence of financial literacy on people's lives. This ebook serves as a platform for me to share my knowledge and insights, aiming to assist individuals in cultivating the financial confidence and security they rightfully deserve. I'm enthusiastic about the prospect of contributing to your financial journey through this resource.

FOREWORD

It can be difficult to come up with a plan for everything in your life. This is especially true when it comes to making financial plan or budget that will help you achieve financial success. It will be a hard road and you will face many challenges while trying to adhere to a budget but it is well worth it and will prove to be very beneficial in the future.

A lot of people do not know the first thing about budgeting and become very confused when trying to create a budget. If you are one of these people, do not worry, there is hope for you and you can create a budget that works for you. All you need is some guidance and information that will help you along your way.

This book was designed to guide you along your journey to achieving financial success and creating a feasible budget. The following chapters will go over some important steps that you will have to take. It is important to pay attention to all the information that you read as it will most likely be very beneficial for you.

If you are truly serious about getting a hold on your financial situation and beginning a journey to success do not hesitate to read this book!

CHAPTER 1:
BUDGET BASICS

Overview

If you are like most people, you have ups and downs when it comes to your financial situation. In most cases, there are many more down times than up. What if I were to tell you that your situation can be much better than that, would you believe me? Well you should because it is true!

Many people often hinder their own financial success because they own mentality gets in the way. They may think that success is not possible and therefore they in fact make it impossible. The mind is very powerful so you must think positively while trying to achieve financial success and goodness will come your way.

Achieving financial success can be done a lot easier than you probably think it can. If you are determined and know what you want in life you will surely be able to do it. It is important that you know however that the first and most important step in achieving financial success is creating a budget. The following chapter will go over the basics of creating a budget. In this chapter you will find some helpful information that will help you as well as some tips on budgeting. The information provided is quite useful so make sure to pay close attention.

The Basics

Before you will be able to reach financial success you will have to understand a few things. We will begin with the basics of creating a budget. The basics are what will serve as your foundation. It is important that you have a very strong understanding of these basics to ensure that you have a strong foundation.

The following information will shed light on the basics for you. Keep in mind that some information will be explained in greater detail later on in this book.

Determine What Your Current Financial Situation Is:

If you want to create a budget that works for you it is important that you take the time to determine what your current financial situation is. You must be honest with yourself during this process, no matter how difficult it may be. You cannot make your situation seem better than it is, if it is bad you must accept it. Realizing how bad your financial situation is may be the motivator that you need to create a budget. People often do no change their behaviors until there is a reason to do so. Determining your current financial situation may be the reason that helps you change your ways.

Determine What Your Financial Future Looks Like:

While trying to create a budget it is important to consider what your financial future will look like if you do not create a budget for yourself. You really need to try hard to visualize what your life will be like if you do not get your finances in order. Think of what your family may go through and the hard times that they will all have to face. What if sometime in the future you cannot even put food on the table? What if that time in the future is sooner than you think?

These visualizations and thoughts will likely be a motivator to help you change and create a budget. I may be scary to think about it but it can become a reality so it is important to acknowledge the fact that it can become real and change your future.

Figure Out How Much Money You Want:

It is important for you to set financial goals for yourself because they will help you stick to your budget. Do not try to set an exact figure of money as your goal. Instead you want to try to come up with a general number. This number will serve as your gauge to let you know if you are pulling in enough finances. Picking an exact number is a sure way to drive someone crazy and set them up for failure. Having a general number is much more beneficial because it can let someone know when they pull in more than they were expecting while at the same time lets them know if they fall behind and pull in less than what was expected.

Be Realistic:

When trying to create a budget for yourself it is important that you always remain reasonable and that you are realistic with yourself. Do not make an outrageous budget that you cannot follow. This is a sure way to set yourself up for failure and feel like you are not capable of following any budget.

Keep in mind, you may have to create different budgets as the time goes by. You will want to start with a less complicated budget that will be easier for you to follow. Once you have been able to follow this budget without setbacks it is time to move on to more complicated and strict budgets.

Before you know it you will be budgeting at ease and all of life's benefits will be flooding into your life.

CHAPTER 2: RECORD YOUR INCOME

Overview

As mentioned before, when making a budget one of the most important steps is figuring out what your current financial situation is. You need to figure out the exact number of all income that you have. This can sometimes be a difficult process for people, especially those who are not good with numbers or have multiple forms of income to keep track of.

If you are a person who is not sure of how to or has difficulties when trying to figure out your exact income, this chapter is meant for you. Do not feel overwhelmed! Yes, it may be a difficult process and be quite stressful, but with proper tips and the useful information this next chapter will provide you with, financial success is right around the corner.

Continue reading to learn more about recording your income, its importance, and how you can do it.

Figure Out What You Make

If you want to create a functional budget that is beneficial for you the first thing that you have to do is figure out know much money you make on a monthly basis. It is advised that you do this with a calculator or a number machine because there will be many numbers involved and you want the calculations to be exact. As well, using a calculator or number machine will make this process much less stressful which is good for anyone. This is especially true with a number machine because it prints out the calculations as they are made which can allow a person to make notes or easily review the information.

You need to factor in all forms of income, no matter how small they may be. A lot of people make the mistake of short changing their selves while doing this step because they may think that certain forms of income are too small to count. All forms of income must be counted; cutting yourself short can completely mess up your budget. All the small things add up so make sure to count them!

The following steps will help you to figure out what your exactly monthly income is:

Calculate The Amount In Your Liquid Accounts:

A liquid account is a general term and can include many different types of accounts. It basically refers to any type of account that you can draw money from on a moments notice. The account may include your savings account, your checking account, as well as your investment account. While checking how much is in each one of these accounts it is important for you to remember that some of these accounts build interest and that some may have expenses attached to them. This must also be factored in to your numbers as it will make a big difference while making your budget, even if it does not seem like it now.

Figure Out Your Exact Monthly Income:

The next thing you need to do is figure out what your exact monthly income is. As mentioned before, this can be more difficult for some compared to others for many different reasons. Maybe they have more than one form of income or maybe they get confused by math, either way it can be quite complicated for them. Keep in mind, this is not usually an easy process for any person but it can and must be done.

For those who work on hourly wages you will begin by figuring out what your hourly pay is and then multiplying it by the number of hours you work each week. For those who have varied schedules it is advised that you use the hours from the lowest week instead of the highest because it will prevent you from falling short in the future. Once you have done this you multiply that number by four because there are four weeks in a month. The number you calculate will be your total monthly income, that wasn't that hard right?

For those who work on salary wages you will need to figure out how much you make on a monthly basis instead of yearly. This is because it is much easier to stick to and create a monthly budget rather than an annual one.

All you will have to do is take your total yearly income and divide it by twelve. The figure you come up with will be your total monthly income.

For those who work odd jobs or do not have regular work this process can be a little more difficult. What you need to do if you are one of these people is come up with an average amount of income for the past six months to a year. It is advised that you use a month that had hard times so that you allow yourself breathing room while you create your budget.

It is important to remember to factor in all other forms of extra income as well. Any amount needs to be factored in, no matter how small it may be. This is because you need to be very precise while figuring out how much money you pull in on a monthly basis. Everything from alimony to child support needs to be considered. Even something as small as cash back on credit card purchases needs to be accounted for in your list of earnings.

CHAPTER 3: MAKE A LIST OF EXPENSES AND PUT THEM IN CATEGORIES

Overview

The next step that you must take if you want to create to a beneficial budget is to make a list of all of your expenses and put them into categories. Just like when you were making your list of income, you must include all expenses no matter how small you may think they are. The small things add up after a while and before you know it they can overrule your budget.

This step may be a little bit more complicated than the previous one of listing your income. This is due to the fact that you will likely have many more forms or expenses than you will forms on income. This will likely be a process that will take a bit of time to complete. It is important that while listing your expenses you are precise and take your time, cutting corners will almost surely lead to failure of your budget.

The following chapter will provide you with some tips and information that will make your experience with determining your expenses much less stressful and much easier.

What Are You Spending?

Now that you have determined what your exact monthly income is, it is time for you to begin figuring out what your monthly expenses are and to sort them into different categories. Sorting your expenses into different categories will help you with determining which expenses can be cut, we will go deeper in detail with this step in the chapter following this one.

No matter how difficult the process may be or how frustrated you get while doing it, it is important that you do this step. You must make sure that you are not spending more money on a monthly basis than you are bringing in. While making your list of expenses you will likely be shocked by the final number that you come up with. It is most likely much higher than it needs to be.

The following steps will serve as your guide through this process and make things much easier on you:

Figure Out What You Owe Each Month In Debt:

You need to determine what you spend each month on debts. This can include items such as car loans, title loans, credit cards, student loans, personal loans, and any other form of debt that you may have. This is extremely important to do if you want to get yourself out of a hole and better your financial situation. It is important to list down each item as well as total them all together.

Remember To Include Monthly Insurance Payments:

It is important to make sure that your things are protected in life but at the same time it also important to make sure that you have the money to pay for this protection. When you create your list of expenses you need to make sure to include all of your monthly insurance expenses. If you pay for your insurance quarterly or annually you need to divide the amount of your payment by the appropriate number so you can determine its monthly cost. Common forms of insurance people have is car insurance and homeowners insurance.

Calculate Your Monthly Utility Bills:

Utility bills must also be accounted for in your list of expenses. You cannot really figure out an exact number while doing this because your utility bills will be slightly different from month to month, especially during season changes. You need to figure out how much all of your utility bills were for the past three months and then calculate the average bill amount for those three months. Examples of utility bills are electricity, gas, and phone bills.

Figure Out What You Spend Each Month On Groceries:

We all need to eat so we all have grocery bills. As well, we all know how expensive groceries can be. Even generic brand items seem like they are getting more and more expensive every day. It is extremely important while listing your expenses that you remember to include your average monthly expenses on groceries. Just like with utilities, your monthly grocery expenses will likely differ so you cannot get an exact number but you can get an average. You may find that you need to switch to cheaper brands or lay off of some items for a while.

Remember Special Occasions:

While listing down all of your expenses it is important that you remember to factor in special occasions. Events such as birthdays or certain holidays can end up being quite expensive. When you make purchases for these occasions it is important that you keep the receipts so that it is easier for you to include these expenses in your list.

Study Your Previous Cash Withdrawals:

You need to make sure that you include all of your cash withdrawals that went to various different things. You need to look at your bank statement and figure out the amount of your withdrawals and then list them down along with the reason the money was spent.

Once you have made this list it is time to move on to the next step in your journey. Continue reading to learn more valuable information.

CHAPTER 4: TOTAL EVERYTHING AND MAKE ADJUSTMENTS TO SPENDING

Overview

While making your list of monthly expenses you likely made some very shocking discoveries. Were you spending more money each month than you thought? Do not worry if you were because this is quite common. Not that you have come to this realization it is time for you to begin thinking about if certain changes need to take place. It can be quite easy to feel the need for expensive things that really are not necessary, but you have to ask yourself if you really need them.

The following chapter will go over the importance of getting rid of some of the financial burdens in your life and cutting down others. It will also provide you with some valuable tips that will help you to get rid of the things you do not need.

Get Rid Of Unnecessary Expenses

It seems like in today's society you have to spend money on unnecessary things in order to be able to fit in. For example, everywhere you look you will be sure to see a teenager with an iPhone or some other smart phone. The kids that do not have one are considered to be outsiders and are not accepted by their peers. Although it may seem like a necessary expense to go get an iPhone, it really isn't.

Now that you have made your list of your monthly expenses and your monthly income it is time to start comparing the two lists with one another. If you ever plan on getting ahead in life you must make sure that you are pulling in more money than you are spending, it's only common sense. This doesn't mean that you make two dollars more a month than your expenses total up to. It means that you should have substantial breathing room because unexpected things happen in life and you may make less money during one month than others. If you are spending more money each month than you take in you are in a bad spot and your surely know it and can feel the consequences. It can feel like you are stuck in a black hole with no way out. The power of the hole continues to suck you deeper and deeper in until you can no longer see light and can no longer manage your debts.

If you want to adhere to a budget and create a financial success for your life you will likely have to give up certain activities and go without certain things in life for a while. Ask almost anyone who has achieved financial success and was not just born into a rich family, they will surely tell you that they had to make many sacrifices. You have to determine what is essential in your life and what are just mere desires. Knowing the difference between the two is extremely important as it will help you to make difficult decisions about your finances in the future. No matter how big the temptation or urge may be it is important not to spend compulsively and to adhere to your budget. After all, it was designed and created by you for you.

The following are some examples of the things you may not want to go without but need to for financial reasons for a while:

Cable TV:

You need to ask yourself if this is really a necessity in your life. How much is your bill and how much do you really watch it?

Going Out:

You may need to limit going out for a while or at least restrict where you go or the amount of money you take with you. It is advised that you stay away from high priced places while trying to stick to a budget because these places are a set up for failure. Going to clubs and high priced restaurants will get you nothing but an empty wallet and over-priced food that is often times over rated. Stick to places that are a bit cheaper. Try going bowling or going out to a pool hall to play a couple games. No matter what your interest are you should be able to find something cheaper to do that will entertain you and keep you inside of the lines of your budget.

Eat At Home More:

Many people do not realize how expensive it can be to eat out

KENNISHA PRESSLEY-SMITH M.ED.

constantly. A few bucks a meal may not seem expensive at the time of your purchase but it definitely adds up quite quickly. You can prepare the same meals you get at restaurants in your own kitchen. Even if you are not great at cooking you can learn. The same meal you can get from a restaurant can be prepared at home for a fraction of the price. This is beneficial for your health as well as your budget. One thing to keep in mind as well is that your health is extremely important for achieving any type of success, including financial success so eat healthy!

Cancel Unnecessary Subscriptions:

A lot of people sign up for a magazine subscription or newspaper subscription with every intention of looking at them and reading them everyday. For some people this ends up being the case but for a lot of people it ends up being the exact opposite. The magazines just sit around and collect dust or some people may still have newspapers from last year around their house. When you think about it, wasting money on something that does nothing more than sit around and collect dust seems kind of foolish. The money being spent on those subscriptions could go to other valuable things. Even if you do read the magazine, do you really need it?

Magazines and newspapers are just a couple examples of the countless subscriptions that a person can have.

Cancel Unnecessary Memberships:

Just as with subscriptions, you need to determine if certain memberships you pay for are necessary and healthy for your budget. For example, if you pay for a membership to a grocery store like Sam's Club or Costco but have not been there in quite a while, it is probably a good idea to cancel those memberships. Another example may be if you are in some other type of club like a car club. You may have to make the sacrifice of leaving the club and suspending your membership until you can better afford the membership fees.

These are just a few examples of the things that you may have to slow down on or cut out completely to be able to stick to your budget and achieve financial success. Nobody said that every step of the process of creating a budget would be easy. I can guarantee you one thing though, it will be beneficial for your life in the long run. It is important to find a way to still leave yourself some joys in life while sticking to a budget. It is as the saying goes, "all work and no play makes Jack a dull boy". This is entirely true and working without rewards can eventually completely destroy a person's motivation to do something. This will likely lead to you abandoning your budget entirely. That would mean that all of the hard work and effort you put into getting this far with your budget would have been for absolutely nothing. So keep that in mind and always remember that you still need to enjoy life!

CHAPTER 5: REVIEW REGULARLY

Overview

When you have finally constructed a complete budget for yourself it is important to make a hard copy of it. As a matter of fact you may want to make several hard copies. This is because you need to look over your budget on a regular basis. This will not only help you to stay on track but it will serve as a motivator as well you help you keep fighting for a better financial future. As well, it is important to have hard copies of your budget because as time goes on your budget will likely change.

The following chapter will explain why it is important to review your budget on a regular basis and some tips that can help you remember to do so.

Take Time To Look Over Your Budget

It is important that you look over your budget on a frequent basis. It should really be done every time you have a chance. This is because a hard copy of your budget is very helpful in determining if you are sticking to it or not.

You need to put a copy of your budget in places that you spend a lot of your time. You may even want to try hanging one on a wall in your room or putting a copy on the front of your refrigerator. One place that you will surely see it every day is if you tape it to your bathroom mirror. While you are getting ready to start your day you will see this budget and it will keep it fresh in your mind.

It may be easy for us to forget some things in our life, especially those things that we don't really want to remember, such as budgets. Constantly reviewing you budget will make it much more difficult for you to forget about it, intentional or not. It will be easier for you to avoid impulse spending as well because you will think of your budget while you look at the price tag of a certain object. You will understand that in order to get that object you will have to get rid of other expenses so that you do not go above your budget. The choice of whether it is worth it or not is up to you.

Another reason that you need to look over your budget as much as possible is to make sure that it does not need to be revised or have changes made to it. As mentioned earlier in this book, you will likely start with a simple budget and move up to a more difficult one. If you do not look over your budget and realize that you are ready to move on to a more difficult one you will be stuck in the same rut forever. As well, you may get a new job which offers more or less income so changes to your budget will be necessary.

One thing that you may want to try is to draw a little picture or write out a statement on your budget that describes the reason you are doing it. This will surely keep the benefits of your struggles at the front of your mind and make continuing on with your budget much easier. Remember, much of this process is determination and hard work, without the two you will get nowhere!

WRAPPING UP

Creating and following a budget can be quite difficult; I will not lie to you. It is possible though as long as you stick to your guns and remain strong. As stated before, always keep in mind the benefits that you are receiving from sticking to your budget. This will surely help to keep you motivated and to continue on with your fight for financial security and success.

If you have difficulties at first with following your budget, do not be discouraged. Most people find it very difficult to follow a budget at the beginning but noticed that it gets easier as time goes by and wallets get fatter. If you want to achieve financial success you will surely have to give many things up but they will be replaced with a secure future and wealth beyond what you ever imagined you would have.

Most wealthy people did not start out that way. They had to work hard like everyone else to get where they are. Most of them had to make sacrifices to get them to the point that they are at. Ask anyone of them if they spend impulsively, even though they have the money to do so they will likely say no. This is because it is these types of decisions that got them to the wealth thcy havc in the first place. They understand that what is earned can be spent, and twice as fast.

If you follow your budget it will not be long before you begin to see the results that it will bring. Your life will get better and you will feel less stressed out. You will be able to enjoy the smaller things in life again and will not be constantly making yourself sick over bills and other expenses anymore.

It will be hard but you can do it, I believe in you! I hope this book has been helpful for you and I hope you are able to stick to your budget and achieve financial success. Good luck!

BUDGET WORKSHEET

MONTHLY BUDGET

MONTH OF				
TOTAL INCOME		OTHER INCOME / SAVINGS		
EXPENSES ITEM	**BUDGET**	**ACTUAL**	**DIFFERENCE**	**NOTES**
MORTGAGE/RENT				
HOUSEHOLD MAINTENANCE				
TAXES				
INSURANCE				
ELECTRICITY				
WATER				
SEWAGE				
GAS				
PHONE				
TRASH				
CABLE				
CELL PHONE				
GROCERIES				
ENTERTAINMENT				
CHARITY/DONATIONS				
FUEL				
AUTO INSURANCE				
CAR PAYMENT				
CHILD CARE				
CREDIT CARDS/DEBT				
LOANS				
DINING OUT				
SPORTING EVENTS				
LIVE THEATER				
CONCERTS				
MOVIES				
TOTAL EXPENSES				

www.ingramcontent.com/pod-product-compliance
Lightning Source LLC
Chambersburg PA
CBHW050528290526
45786CB00007B/2734